8x (2/12) ✓4/13

4X $\dfrac{9/10}{1/11}$

Stories of GREAT PEOPLE

Queen Victoria's diamond

Gerry Bailey and Karen Foster

Illustrated by Leighton Noyes
and Karen Radford

🍄 Crabtree Publishing Company

www.crabtreebooks.com

DIGBY PLATT is an antique collector. Every Saturday he picks up a bargain at Mr. Rummage's antique stall and loves listening to the story behind his new "find".

HANNAH PLATT is Digby's argumentative, nine year-old sister—and she doesn't believe a word that Mr. Rummage says!

Mr. RUMMAGE has a stall piled high with interesting objects—and he has a great story to tell about each and every one of his treasures.

PIXIE the market's fortuneteller sells incense, lotions and potions, candles, mandalas, and crystals inside her exotic stall.

Crabtree Publishing Company
www.crabtreebooks.com

Other books in the series

Armstrong's moon rock
Cleopatra's coin
Columbus's chart
Galileo's telescope
Julius Caesar's sandals
Leonardo's palette
Marco Polo's silk purse
Martin Luther King Jr.'s microphone
Mother Teresa's alms bowl
Mozart's wig
Shakespeare's quill
Sitting Bull's tomahawk
The Wright Brothers' glider

Credits

Bettmann/Corbis: p. 9, 21 (top); Michael St Maur Sheil: p. 21 (bottom)

Hulton Archive/Getty Images: p. 33 (top)

Mary Evans Picture Library: p. 17, 19

Topfoto: p. 23, 28; British Library, London/HIP: p. 13 (bottom left);
    City of London/HIP: p. 13 (bottom right); Museum of London/HIP:
    p. 15 (bottom); Picturepoint: p. 10, 15 (top), 25, 31 (top), 33 (bottom), 35;
    World History Archive: p. 13 (top), 29 (bottom), 31 (bottom)

Corporation of London/HIP/Topham: p. 27 (top), 29 (top)

Picture research: Diana Morris. info@picture-research.co.uk
Editor: Lynn Peppas
Proofreaders: David Hurd, Crystal Sikkens
Project editor: Robert Walker
Prepress technician: Ken Wright
Production coordinator: Margaret Amy Salter

Library and Archives Canada Cataloguing in Publication

Bailey, Gerry
    Queen Victoria's diamond / Gerry Bailey and Karen
Foster ; illustrated by Leighton Noyes and Karen Radford.

(Stories of great people)
Includes index.
ISBN 978-0-7787-3697-4 (bound).--ISBN 978-0-7787-3719-3 (pbk.)

    1. Victoria, Queen of Great Britain, 1819-1901--Juvenile fiction.
2. Queens--Great Britain--Biography--Juvenile fiction. 3. Great
Britain--History--Victoria, 1837-1901--Juvenile fiction. 4. Victoria,
Queen of Great Britain, 1819-1901--Juvenile literature. 5. Queens--Great
Britain--Biography--Juvenile literature. 6. Great Britain--History--
Victoria, 1837-1901--Juvenile literature. I. Noyes, Leighton II. Radford,
Karen III. Foster, Karen, 1959- IV. Title. V. Series.

PZ7.B15Qu 2008   j823'.92   C2008-907336-3

Library of Congress Cataloging-in-Publication Data

Bailey, Gerry.
    Queen Victoria's diamond / Gerry Bailey and Karen Foster ; illustrated
by Leighton Noyes and Karen Radford.
        p. cm. -- (Stories of great people)
    Includes index.
    ISBN 978-0-7787-3719-3 (pbk. : alk. paper) -- ISBN 978-0-7787-3697-4
(reinforced lib. bdg. : alk. paper)
    1. Victoria, Queen of Great Britain, 1819-1901--Juvenile literature. 2.
Queens--Great Britain--Biography--Juvenile literature. 3. Great
Britain--History--Victoria, 1837-1901--Juvenile literature. I. Foster,
Karen, 1959- II. Noyes, Leighton, ill. III. Radford, Karen, ill. IV.
Title. V. Series.

    DA557.B355 2008
    941.081092--dc22
    [B]
                                    2008048637

Crabtree Publishing Company
www.crabtreebooks.com   1-800-387-7650

Published in Canada
Crabtree Publishing
616 Welland Ave.
St. Catharines, Ontario
L2M 5V6

Published in the United States
Crabtree Publishing
PMB16A
350 Fifth Ave., Suite 3308
New York, NY 10118

Published by CRABTREE PUBLISHING COMPANY
Copyright © **2009** Diverta Ltd.

Queen Victoria's diamond
Table of Contents

Every Saturday morning, Knicknack Market comes to life. The street vendors are there almost before the sun is up. And by the time you and I are out of bed, the stalls are built, the boxes are opened, and all the goods are carefully laid out on display.

Objects are piled high. Some are laid out on velvet: precious necklaces and jeweled swords. Others stand upright at the back: large, framed pictures of very important people, lamps made from tasseled satin, and old-fashioned cash registers—the kind that jingle when the drawers are opened.

And then there are things that stay in their boxes all day, waiting for the right customer to come along: war medals laid out in straight lines, stopwatches on leather straps, and utensils in polished silver for all those special occasions.

But Mr. Rummage's stall is different. Mr. Rummage of Knicknack Market has a stall piled high with a disorderly jumble of things that no one could ever want. Who'd want to buy a stuffed mouse? Or a broken umbrella? Or a pair of false teeth?

Well, Mr. Rummage has them all. And, as you can imagine, they don't cost a lot!

Digby Platt—ten-year-old collector of antiques—was off to see his friend Mr. Rummage of Knicknack Market. It was Saturday and, as usual, Digby's weekly allowance was burning a hole in his pocket.

Digby wasn't going to spend it on any old thing. It had to be something rare and interesting for his collection, something from Mr. Rummage's incredible stall. Hannah, his older sister, had come along too. She had secret doubts about the value of Mr. Rummage's objects and felt, for some big-sisterly reason, that she had to stop her little brother from buying useless junk.

As they rounded the corner, they saw that Mr. Rummage was chatting with Pixie, from the New Age tent down the street.

"Hello Mr. Rummage, hello Pixie," chorused the children.

"Hi kids. You've arrived just in time to look at this," said Pixie, opening the palm of her hand to reveal a tiny but perfectly formed crystal.

"Wow!" said Hannah, as the crystal twinkled brightly in the sunlight.

"Where did you get that from?"

"From my Queen Victoria collection," said Mr. Rummage proudly.

"I bet it's worth millions," said Digby excitedly. "Can I hold it, Pixie?"

"OK Digby, but be careful you don't drop it." Mr. Rummage took out a very old diamond cutter's eyeglass and let the children look at the beautiful stone.

"It's very small, of course," Mr. Rummage began, "but I'm told it was once part of the huge Indian Koh-i-noor diamond that was presented to Queen Victoria herself! The Koh-i-noor was re-cut specially for her, and this is probably a chip that fell off the royal jeweler's cutting block." "Ugh, bad joke!" groaned Digby and Hannah. "Alright," laughed Mr.Rummage, "let me tell you a bit about Queen Victoria anyway. She didn't like jokes much either, from what I can gather."

 # Queen Victoria

Victoria was born on May 24, 1819. Her father was Edward, Duke of Kent. Her mother was Princess Victoria of Saxe-Coberg-Saalfeld in what is now Germany. Unfortunately for Victoria, her father died when she was just eight-months-old, leaving her mother penniless and in debt.

The Victorian Age

Nevertheless, Victoria became Queen of England when she was just 18 years old. She was known for her hard work, her sense of duty, and her belief in strong family values. Over the years she became the symbol of a peaceful and wealthy nation. Her 63-year **reign** is known as the **Victorian Age**. She ruled during a time of great change, new ideas, and discoveries in science and technology. By the time she died in 1901, she had reigned longer than any other British **monarch** before her.

But let's find out more...

Life in Kensington Palace

The Royal Steward, Sir John Conroy, and Victoria's mother kept a close eye on Victoria: She was never allowed to be on her own, and could not meet anyone unless someone was in the room with her. Conroy chose Victoria's teachers, and organized every tiny detail of her daily routine. Her mother made sure she was not hidden away altogether. It was important that Victoria's future subjects knew who she was, and the little girl was often seen playing or riding her donkey in the royal gardens at Kensington Palace.

A strict education

Victoria's mother hired a strict **governess**, called Louise Lehzen, to teach her daughter. Luckily, Victoria was very bright and excellent at languages, although she did have some trouble with Latin. She spent hours drawing and reading history books. She also loved music and learned to dance, which made her graceful and dignified—something she became well known for. In case that wasn't enough, Victoria's governess tied a sprig of prickly holly under her chin to encourage her to hold her head up in a queenly fashion!

A portrait of Princess Victoria and her mother.

Lonely princess

Victoria had no playmates of her own age, but she did have a fabulous collection of dolls and puppets that kept her company. Her dolls were made of wax or china and dressed in satin, taffeta, or lace.

"How could Victoria have become Queen if she had no money?" asked Digby. "I thought people with debts were thrown into prison in those days."

"Victoria was royal, and royals are treated differently, silly," said Hannah, snootily.

"Luckily, her favorite uncle, Leopold, came to her rescue," said Mr. Rummage. "He helped Victoria's mother out so that her little girl could be brought up like a future queen."

"So Leopold was a sort of father figure, then?" said Pixie.

"In a way," said Mr. Rummage, "he told Princess Victoria she must always do her duty. He also warned her only to trust loyal servants—and never to answer a question until she'd thought it over first."

"He doesn't sound much fun to me," said Digby.

"No, but he probably meant well," said Mr. Rummage. "Unlike Sir John Conroy—he was a completely different kettle of fish altogether."

"Why, what did he do?" asked Digby.

"Well, Conroy was the royal **steward**. He was greedy and ambitious and ruled the royal household with a rod of iron. He charmed Victoria's mother to get her favor, then made her afraid of what might happen if she didn't keep an eye on her daughter all the time."

"What was the point in that?" asked Hannah. "I think he believed that if Victoria became Queen, he would have power over her. But instead, Victoria hated him for taking away her freedom."

"No wonder. He sounds really strict," said Hannah.

"Yes," agreed Mr. Rummage, "but her mother didn't help. She ordered her footmen to watch Victoria while she was playing, and made her sleep in her bedroom every night until she became queen!"

"Poor Victoria," said Digby. "I feel sorry for her already."

"I bet Victoria could hardly wait to be Queen," said Hannah. "All that pampering must have been awful."

"Actually, she didn't know she was going to be Queen until she was 11," said Mr. Rummage. "One day she was reading a history book when she came across a picture of the Royal Family Tree. Only then did she realize she was next in line for the throne."

"What a shock!" said Digby. "Imagine opening a book and reading that you're going to rule a country."

"Indeed, my boy, and the poor girl was very upset about it," said Mr. Rummage. "Apparently she raised her hand and promised her teacher, 'I will be good,' before bursting into tears."

"But didn't she still have a long time to wait?" asked Hannah.

"She did," agreed Mr. Rummage. "It wasn't until June 20, 1837 that King William died. Victoria was woken up by her mother at six o'clock in the morning and sent downstairs to the sitting room.

There, still in her dressing gown, she was told that she was to be crowned Queen. Three hours later, Viscount Melbourne—who was a bit like today's Prime Minister—knelt down and kissed her hand."

"I bet after so many years of being told what to do, she was glad to have her freedom," laughed Hannah.

"She was," agreed Pixie. "And one of the first things she did as queen was give her mother a new bedroom—at the other end of the house!"

"I don't blame her," said Digby, as everyone laughed.

Coronation Day

Victoria was driven in a glittering procession to Westminster Abbey, through streets crammed with cheering people waving flags. As her golden coach drew up, a spectator wrote that she was dressed in a beautiful white satin gown, with eight ladies-in-waiting floating around her like a silvery cloud. Apparently, when the crown was put on her head, a ray of sunlight fell on her in a magical moment, and everyone gasped at her good luck. After the banquet, she watched a firework display from her royal balcony, as Londoners celebrated in fairgrounds and theaters all over the city. That night, Victoria wrote in her diary: "I shall ever remember this day as the PROUDEST of my life!"

Victoria was crowned in London on June 28th, 1838.

Lord M

William Lamb, Viscount Melbourne, became another father figure to the young queen. He guided her through the first anxious moments of her reign. He told her that it did not matter that she was small and shy, because people would love her for it, and want to protect her. William also explained affairs of state to her and led her gently through her queenly duties. They would conduct state business in the morning and then go horseback riding with the court in the afternoon. Victoria called William - Lord M- and because they were always together, she became known as Mrs. Melbourne.

Princess Victoria was driven through the streets of London in a golden coach.

This Penny Black is one of the very first postage stamps ever to be made. Since Victoria's reign, it has not been necessary to put the name of the country—England—on the stamp. All that is needed is a picture of the monarch's head!

"She didn't stay Mrs. Melbourne for long though," said Pixie. "The real love of her life was her cousin, Prince Albert of Saxe-Coburg-Gotha, the son of a German Duke."

"Albert!" shrieked Hannah. "What a stuffy name! Was he good looking?"

"He certainly set Victoria's heart racing," smiled Pixie. "In fact, she thought he was very handsome, with beautiful eyes."

"Yuck!" exclaimed Digby with a grimace.

"They first met when they were 16," Mr. Rummage went on, "and enjoyed each other's company. Their grandmother and Victoria's mother thought they were a good match. But King William, who was still alive then, had other ideas and tried to stop the cousins from meeting. Eventually, the women's matchmaking won William over."

"Good for them," said Hannah. "But what did Victoria think of Albert?"

"At first she thought he was short and fat. But as she got to know him, she realized he was polite, friendly, and very smart."

"He sounds a bit boring to me," said Digby.

"Well," said Pixie, "Victoria was so smitten, she said she'd refuse to marry anyone if she couldn't have him."

"When Albert returned to England some time after," said Mr. Rummage, "he'd grown up and looked every inch the romantic prince. Victoria lost no time in proposing marriage to him herself."

"She proposed!" cried Digby. "I thought he was supposed to do that."

"Oh no," replied Mr. Rummage, "no one is allowed to propose to the Queen of England. She had to do it herself!"

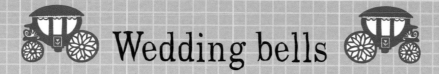

Wedding bells

Prince Albert

Queen Victoria and Prince Albert married in 1840 at St. James's Palace, London. Albert was an intelligent young man—he was fascinated by science, loved art, and was also talented in music, fencing, and riding. However, he was often sickly and seemed very serious. Albert was in a difficult position. He worked very hard as Victoria's private secretary, but he was not as popular as his wife. Most of his good works in social welfare, trade, and industry were thought to be Victoria's doing, and he was not really appreciated. It was not until 1857 that he was properly recognized by the nation and awarded the title Prince Consort.

Lots of children

Like many women in her day, Queen Victoria produced lots of children. She had nine in all, and by the end of her reign had 37 great grandchildren! Victoria enjoyed having a large family and arranging their domestic life—although she didn't spend much time with them. In Victorian times children were to be "seen and not heard" and were brought up by governesses.

A happy marriage

When Victoria was pregnant, Albert took on many of her duties. Although Albert never became king, he behaved like one. And although Victoria was Queen, she behaved like a dutiful wife, which was expected in those days. She always took his advice and treated him as head of the family.

Victoria and Albert's marriage set an example for the rest of society.

"Where did Victoria and Albert live?" asked Digby.

"Victoria had many homes," said Mr. Rummage. "She had Buckingham Palace, of course, then she had Windsor Castle, Balmoral Castle in Scotland, and Osborne House on the Isle of Wight."

"Lucky thing!" said Hannah. "Were they all given to her?"

"No," replied Mr. Rummage. "She bought Osborne House as a family home in 1845, while Albert bought Balmoral seven years later. They wanted places where they could escape from public attention."

"They also wanted to be safe," added Pixie. "There had been several assassination attempts on the Queen and they'd probably made her feel a bit shaky."

"Anyway," Mr. Rummage went on, "Victoria loved to spend time in her various homes. Apparently they were fitted with all the latest technology when it became available. There were water closets, or toilets, electric lights, and telephone lines."

"But she didn't really like modern conveniences," said Pixie. "According to some people, she hated electric lights and refused to have them in her private apartments. She said they were, 'very inefficient.' Still, the general public didn't realize how old-fashioned she was, because whenever she sent a **telegraph** message to someone or pressed a button to set off a salute of cannon shots, she became a powerful symbol of the new industrial age!" said Mr. Rummage.

The Victorian household

Buckingham Palace

Queen Victoria was the first monarch to use Buckingham Palace as her London home. She moved in three weeks after taking the throne. At first, she thought the palace was dirty because of its smoking chimneys and smelly gas lamps. Then she complained it was too small for her growing family. So Prince Albert arranged to move the Marble Arch between the north and south wings of the palace to Hyde Park, and a new wing was added to make room for the royal nursery and a state ballroom. The building was finished in 1847.

Buckingham House before it became Buckingham Palace, 1809.

The Butler looked after the family's silverware, china, and table linen. He also served at the table and answered the door to callers. The lady's maid helped the mistress of the house with her toilette—which meant getting her dressed. She also looked after her wardrobe, making sure everything from lacy **petticoats** to feather hats was in perfect order.

Royal servants

In Victorian times, all households except for the very poorest had servants to do the everyday work. The royal household was packed with people, who cleaned, cooked, and looked after the children.

The valet was personal secretary to the master of the house. He also looked after his clothes, polished his boots and the buttons on his coats, and brushed his hats. The footman cleaned and filled the oil lamps and polished the silver and copper. He often did the shopping, while the cook prepared all the meals for the household and made sure the food in the larder was fresh.

"Victoria and Albert must have spent a lot of their time traveling from one country house to another. I bet that was fun," said Digby.

"No it wasn't," sniffed Hannah. "Traveling was really uncomfortable then, especially if the weather was bad, wasn't it Mr Rummage?"

"Well, it was improving," said Mr. Rummage. "The railway saw to that. In fact, Victoria wrote about the first time she saw a steam train in her diary: 'It passed with surprising quickness, striking sparks as it flew along the railroad, enveloped in clouds of smoke and making a loud noise. It was a curious thing indeed.'"

"Did she get a special train of her own?" asked Digby.

"She certainly did," said Pixie, joining in. "In fact, it was Albert who asked the Great Western Railway to build her a State Railway Carriage. It wasn't big by today's standards, but it was beautifully made in satin wood and bird's eye maple, with a crown on the roof. The inside looked just like a miniature Victorian parlor, with silk and lace curtains, carpets, and decorative furniture."

"That's right," Mr. Rummage went on.

"When they made their first trip on it Victoria said she was 'quite charmed' by it—but Albert worried that the locomotive was going too fast, even though it was only puffing along at 50 miles per hour (80km/h)!" "Sometimes she was shocked by what she saw when she looked out of the train window," said Pixie.

"Especially as they chugged past grim, sooty, industrial towns. She wrote in her diary about 'black buildings flaming with fire, smoking and burning coal heaps, wretched huts and carts, and little ragged children.'"

"She probably felt guilty she had such a comfortable life," suggested Digby.

"You may be right Digby," said Mr. Rummage. "But I expect she soon forgot all about it because at every station stop, cannons fired salutes, choirs sang the national anthem, and crowds of people cheered her on."

"Wow!" exclaimed the children open-mouthed.

Transport

Railway fever

The coming of the railways changed the lives of everyone in Victorian Britain. And by 1852 all the main routes in the country had been built. Huge railway stations, including London's Paddington, King's Cross, and Waterloo became symbols of the achievements of the Industrial Revolution in Victorian Britain.

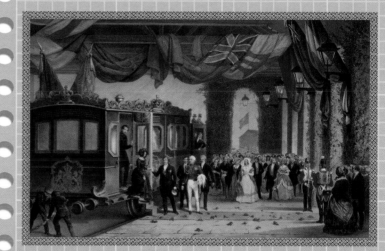

Victoria enjoyed traveling around the country in her royal railway carriage.

Cycling craze

Many Victorians began riding bicycles or three-wheeled tricycles. Fashionable ladies wore special cycling costumes, which must have taken a long time to put on. Magazines of the day recommended a lightly boned blouse or leather vest, a skirt-coat, **knickerbockers**, leggings, low shoes with **spats** (to keep out the gravel), doeskin gloves, and a quill hat. Phew!

"While Queen Victoria was having babies, what was Prince Albert doing?" asked Hannah.

"Well, he wasn't twiddling his thumbs, that's for sure," said Mr. Rummage. "Oh no, he was tinkering with some impressive building and engineering projects—The Great Exhibition at Crystal Palace, for example, was his baby."

"What was the Crystal Palace?" asked Digby. "It sounds like something out of a fairytale."

"It was a huge glass building in Hyde Park," replied Mr. Rummage. "It was large enough to enclose fully-grown trees, fountains, statues, and avenues of display tables. The royal family opened it in May 1851, with spectacular fireworks and a colorful circus."

"I wish I'd been there," sighed Pixie.

"Crystal Palace was an amazing feat of engineering," Mr. Rummage went on. "It was built from hundreds of tons of glass and thousands of iron bars."

"Wow!" gasped Hannah. "Albert must have been very proud of his idea."

"He was," said Mr. Rummage, "although it was designed by a gardener named Paxton."

"A gardener!" cried Digby. "You mean it was a giant greenhouse?"

"More or less," smiled Mr. Rummage. "There were certainly plenty of hot houses packed with rare, exotic plants from all over the world. But, really, the exhibition celebrated amazing inventions in science and industry. It also showed off treasures of the British **Empire** In the end it was visited by over six million people."

The Great Exhibition

A huge success

Much to people's surprise, the exhibition was a huge success and made money. The Natural History Museum, Science museums, and the Victoria and Albert Museum in London were all funded by its profits.

The opening of the Great Exhibition in Hyde Park, London, in 1851.

Victorian curiosities

The Victorian Age was an exciting time of discovery and exploration. Distant, little-known lands were visited and thousands of exotic animals were sent to London to be put on show in museums and zoos, and in the Great Exhibition itself. Victorians became keen collectors. Many had private collections in their homes, filled with stuffed animals, caged birds, botanical gardens in jars, natural history paintings, and curiosities from other countries.

A Victorian treasure trove

At first, people came to Crystal Palace just to say they had been there and to show off. Soon visitors turned up to see all the exhibits and to educate themselves. The Victorian writer Charlotte Bronte wrote: "it may be called a bazaar or a fair, but it is such a bazaar or fair as Eastern genii might have created. It seems as if only magic could have gathered this mass of wealth from the ends of the Earth."

"Victoria must have been very proud of Albert," said Hannah. "It's a pity he died so young." "It was," agreed Pixie. "She'd adored and relied on him so much that when he went she was completely lost without him."

"And ten years of mourning, shut away in her private apartments, didn't go down very well with the British public either," added Mr. Rummage. "They wanted a grand queen who went out and about, someone they could admire, not someone who was always down in the dumps and kept to herself."

"So Victoria became unpopular then," said Hannah sadly.

"She did, but the poor woman was ill with grief. Apparently every bed she slept in had a picture of Albert above the righthand pillow—and at Balmoral, she'd lay out fresh clothes and water for him every evening."

"That's weird!" said Digby.

"Didn't anyone help her?" asked Hannah.

"There was someone she came to depend on: her Scottish attendant called John Brown," replied Pixie. "He kept her company and went riding with her. He waited on her during the day and slept in the room next door at night."

"That's right," agreed Mr. Rummage. "It's odd because he was almost the opposite of Albert in some ways. She loved John's rough manners, his strength, and the sense of security he gave her. She even allowed him to tell her off if he thought she was wrong about something, which she wouldn't have tolerated from anyone else. But she seemed to enjoy the relationship, however odd it seemed to outsiders."

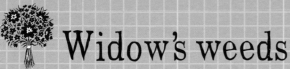

Widow's weeds

After Albert's death in 1861, Victoria spent the rest of her life in widow's weeds, as mourning clothes were called. She was nicknamed the Widow of Windsor. In fact we tend to remember her today, not as a fun-loving young woman, but as a short, plump lady dressed in black velvet, a white widow's cap and heavy pearls.

Queen Victoria wearing a black riding habit. Her black horse is being held by her attendant, John Brown, also dressed in black.

Fashionable black

Victoria's widowhood made black fashionable. People began to use black-edged stationary, envelopes, notepaper, and visiting cards. They tied little black and purple ribbons around perfume bottles and added similar ribbons to their children's clothing. Prayer books and bibles were bound in black morocco leather and lace.

Victoria loses her diamonds

Victoria's uncle Ernest, who later became the King of Hanover, wanted a share of the family fortune. So he made a claim and in 1857 Victoria lost many jewels she had thought were her own. She was so angry, she ordered Garrards, the royal jewelers, to take 28 gemstones from two Garter badges and a sword hilt in the Treasury and make her a new necklace. The central pendant of the "Timur Ruby" necklace, known as the Lahore diamond, was detached so it could be worn on it. Then the sidestones of the famous Indian Koh-i-noor diamond were used to make her a pair of drop earrings, which she later gave to the crown.

"I wish I'd lived at the same time as Victoria," sighed Hannah.

"I'm not sure you'd have liked it that much," said Pixie. "It was fine if you were well off, but children were often forced to go to work when they were a lot younger than you or Digby, so they could earn money for their families."

"What sort of work could children like us do?" asked Digby.

"Well, Hannah might have had to work 12 to 15 hours a day in a cotton mill for not very much money. While you, Digby, might have found yourself down a freezing cold mine, digging for coal, or up a burning hot chimney, sweeping out the soot."

"That's terrible," exclaimed Hannah. "Why didn't anyone do something about it?"

"Some people did. The famous writer Charles Dickens, described the lives of poor children in Victorian London in his books," said Mr. Rummage. "As a result, many Victorians asked themselves if it was right for children to be working at all. Later, laws were made which said what children could and shouldn't do."

Child labor—a harsh life

Millworkers

Many children worked in cotton mills from early morning until late at night. They were forced to clean huge machines while they were still running, so there were many accidents. They were only allowed three meals a day, which they ate standing up, and there was no time to get fresh air or to exercise.

A child working the loom in a cotton mill

Coal mine trappers

Deep down in the coal mines, small children worked the trap doors. They sat in a hole hollowed out for them and pulled a string to open the door when they heard the coal wagons coming. It was not as dangerous as some jobs, but it was dark and lonely.

Match sellers and chimney sweeps

Some children worked on the streets selling matches, They worked long hours for very little money. Other children swept chimneys. Most sweeps came down covered in soot with bleeding elbows and knees. A few, however, got stuck and died of suffocation. In match factories children were employed to dip matches in a dangerous chemical called phosphorus. This made their teeth decay or gave them lung disease.

Charles Dickens

Charles Dickens is famous for his stories about Victorian Britain, where he describes the huge gap between the rich and the poor. Hordes of dirty, ragged children roamed the streets of London with little food and no home to go to. The street children were often orphans with no one to care for them. They stole or picked pockets to buy food, and slept in outhouses or doorways. Dickens wrote about these children in his book, *Oliver Twist*.

"Why did kids prefer to earn factory wages rather than go to school?" asked Digby.

"Schools weren't the comfortable places they are now," smiled Mr. Rummage. "Even so, they were a darn sight better than working down a mine."

"It was the educated Victorians who came up with the idea that everyone should go to school," said Pixie. "They were worried about very poor children growing up unable to read or write. Mind you, the upper classes weren't too happy about the working classes going to school. They were afraid they might get ideas above their **station**."

"There were different kinds of schools," said Mr. Rummage. "One kind was *ragged schools*, where the very poorest children could get some education."

"Why were they called that?" asked Digby.

"Because the children who attended them were so poor they were dressed in rags," said Mr. Rummage. "Younger children might go to a *dame school*, where a local woman would run a classroom in her house. Then there were charity schools, run by local charities, factory schools, where children were taught along with doing their job and, of course, Sunday schools, run by the local church."

Ragged schools

Field Lane Ragged School in London, 1850.

Beads and slates

When Victoria came to the throne paper was expensive, so children in ragged schools wrote on slates with bits of sharpened slate. After a lesson was completed and the teacher checked their work, children cleared their slates ready to begin again. Students were supposed to bring sponges to clean them, but most just spat on the slate and rubbed it clean with a shirt sleeve!

A slate

Large classes

There could be as many as 80 students in one class, especially in the cities. Teachers were very strict. Children were taught by reading and copying things down, or chanting until they were perfect. Discipline was kept with the use of the cane or strap. Today, any kind of physical punishment in schools is against the law.

Student teachers

In many schools, older children helped with the teaching while they learned. Most student teachers were boys or girls of 13 years or older. They could become full-time teachers after a student teacher apprenticeship of five years.

Victorian children's books

Many of today's favorite children's stories were written in Victorian times. *Alice in Wonderland* by Lewis Carroll was a portrait of a middle class girl, while *Mary Poppins*, made the role of the children's governess popular. Other well known books include *Black Beauty*, by Anna Sewell, *What Katy Did*, by Susan Coolidge, *Tom Brown's School Days*, by Thomas Hughes, and *Peter Pan*, by J.M. Barrie.

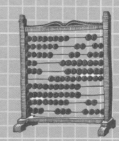

A counting frame

"Did Queen Victoria do anything to help poor people?" asked Digby.

"Well, she did what she could to support charity work and hospitals at home. But she was particularly interested in the work of Florence Nightingale, who took forty nurses to Turkey to look after wounded British soldiers in army hospitals during the Crimean War."

"Florence Nightingale—she's the 'Lady with the Lamp,' isn't she?" said Hannah.

"That's right. It was Florence's strict standards of hygiene and special training that made hospitals cleaner so fewer soldiers died of infection," replied Mr. Rummage. "Victoria always asked to read Miss Nightingale's letters so she could hear the latest news from the warfront, and sent parcels of books, soap, and beef tea to Scutari hospital."

"Did Florence and Victoria ever meet?" asked Hannah.

"They did indeed. When the war was over, the Queen invited her to Balmoral and gave her a brooch to thank her for all her hard work."

Public services

City slums

Victorian cities were very overcrowded. The poorest districts were called slums. Here, smoke and fumes from factory chimneys choked the air, while smelly drains in the streets and dirty drinking water led to fatal diseases like cholera and typhoid. In 1848, public health laws were passed. Gradually, sewers were built, clean water was piped to many homes, and some of the worst slums were pulled down.

Poor families worked together to make ends meet. This family is making matchboxes

Better hospitals

Queen Victoria visited soldiers during wartime and saw the filthy conditions in the military hospitals. She organized relief for the wounded and also awarded the Victoria Cross for bravery. Things improved slowly but surely. The development of antiseptic made surgery safer, and the use of vaccines prevented killer diseases such as tuberculosis and smallpox.

Workhouses

Some well-off Victorians thought the poor did not work hard enough. Old and sick people who could not help themselves were sent to workhouses where they lived in terrible conditions. Families were separated, food was bad, and the work was pointless. Eventually, charities and religious reformers stepped in. They raised money, set up soup kitchens and hostels, and pushed the government to make changes.

The Peelers

Crime was common on the streets of all Victorian cities—from pickpockets to bloody murderers like Jack the Ripper. In 1829, Sir Robert Peel set up a police force in London. The Peelers wore a uniform, so criminals would recognize the police as law enforcers. They wore long, blue "swallow-tail" coats, tall hats, and red waistcoats, which is why they were nicknamed *robin redbreasts*. They also wore leather *Wellington* boots and a leather stock, or collar, that could be quite uncomfortable. It was worn to prevent a criminal with a rope sneaking up behind an officer and strangling him.

A Victorian policeman in a top hat, holding a truncheon.

Charles Dickens wrote about poor children in workhouses in his famous book, *Oliver Twist*. In his story, Oliver caused an uproar by asking for a second helping of porridge while his friends polished their spoons and bowls in their hunger.

"When did Queen Victoria become Empress of India?" asked Hannah.

"She became empress in 1877. That's when India became part of the British Empire." said Mr. Rummage. "Some people said she accepted the title because she was jealous of the **imperial** titles of some of her cousins in Germany and Russia. But I don't think so."

"At least it stopped her mourning," said Hannah. "And she must have enjoyed being head of the biggest empire in the world."

"How big was it?" asked Digby.

"It was said that the Sun never set on Victoria's empire because it was so vast," said Mr. Rummage. "India came to be known as the 'Jewel in the Crown' of the empire. It was run for her by a **Viceroy**, the first of whom was The Earl of Lytton. He wrote to Victoria describing the scene on the plain of Delhi where her title was proclaimed to a huge gathering of princes and noblemen from around India."

"Did they really want a foreigner to be their leader?" asked Digby. "I would have been a bit upset myself."

"I expect lots of the princes didn't. But the British army was strong enough to make the title stick, so they accepted it. Anyway, things were different then. Countries were in the habit of creating little empires for themselves by adding on new lands as they found them."

Jewels in the Crown

Tales of far-off places

With so many foreign lands a part of the British Empire, people began to take an interest in where they were and who lived in them. Many children's books were written that told of adventures in exotic places. *The Jungle Book*, and the *Just So Stories*, by Rudyard Kipling, as well as *Tarzan of the Apes*, by Edgar Rice Burroughs, are just as popular today with young readers as they were then.

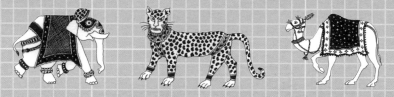

Tiny crown

Queen Victoria was small and found the original Imperial State Crown too heavy and uncomfortable to wear. So she designed and then commissioned a smaller diamond one. The tiny crown is almost four inches (9.9cm) in height and almost three and a half inches (9cm) in diameter. It was made using around 13,000 diamonds from jewelry in her personal collection. Victoria wore it on top of her widow's cap and wore it on many great state occasions. A replica image was stamped on coins and medals she awarded.

Queen Victoria was visited by royal subjects from all over her empire.

"Victoria became very popular with the people of Britain when she was an older lady," explained Pixie. "So Jubilees were held in her honor."

"What's a Jubilee?" asked Digby.

"A celebration," said Pixie, "Victoria had two, held in 1887 and 1897 to celebrate her 50th and 60th anniversary of the longest English reign. The first was called her Golden Jubilee. There was a royal feast in the evening and foreign kings and princes as well as governors of overseas colonies and **dominions** attended."

"In her diary she described eating off gold plates, how beautiful the princesses looked in their ball gowns, and how fine the princes looked in their uniforms," continued Mr. Rummage. "And the next day she traveled in a glittering horse-drawn coach to Westminster Abbey, escorted by the Indian cavalry."

"But she refused to put on her crown, and wore a bonnet instead—can you believe it?" asked Pixie laughing.

Victoria's Jubilees

Diamond Jubilee

The Queen's Diamond Jubilee was celebrated with as much gusto as her Golden one. Over £259,000 ($450,000 U.S. dollars) was spent on street decorations that were lit by gas jets and the newly invented electric light. A film was made of the service at St. Paul's Cathedral but it was very poor in quality. When the Queen sat down to dinner at a table piled high with 60,000 orchid blossoms, 2,500 beacons were lit. Later, she used the newly invented telegraph to broadcast a message of thanks to every part of the empire.

Queen Victoria arrives at St Paul's Cathedral to celebrate her Diamond Jubilee in 1897.

Golden Jubilee banquet

When she had returned to the palace she went out onto the balcony where huge crowds cheered her. Later, in the ballroom, she distributed Jubilee pins to her family. For the evening banquet she put on a splendid gown embroidered with silver roses, thistles, and shamrocks. Afterward she received a long procession of diplomats and Indian princes. The evening ended with a fireworks display that she watched from her chair.

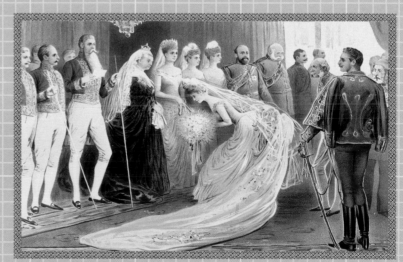

Queen Victoria welcomes guests to her Golden Jubilee reception at Buckingham Palace, 1887.

"I suppose after such a long reign Queen Victoria was quite happy to stay out of the limelight," said Hannah.

"Yes, but she continued to perform her royal duties right to the end," said Mr. Rummage. "She still inspected her troops and visited hospitals."

"And when she died at Osborne House," said Pixie, "the whole country went into mourning."

"What did she die of?" asked Digby. "Was she ill?"

"No, she died of plain old age," replied Mr. Rummage, "stubborn to the end."

"A tough old girl," said Digby.

"Exactly!" said Mr. Rummage.

Queen Victoria's funeral procession

Victoria's death

Victoria died at Osborne House on the Isle of Wight on January 22, 1901. She had reigned for 64 years. The whole country went into mourning and ships sounded their horns as an old-fashioned paddle steamer, the Alberta, carried her coffin to Portsmouth Harbour. From there, she was taken to her final resting place beside her beloved husband Prince Albert at Frogmore Royal Mausoleum. Above the mausoleum door are carved Victoria's words, "...farewell best beloved, here at last I shall rest with thee, with thee in Christ I shall rise again."

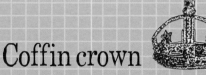

Coffin crown

On her death, the small diamond crown she had made was placed on her coffin at Osborne House. It was later removed to the Tower of London by King George IV, where it can be seen today.

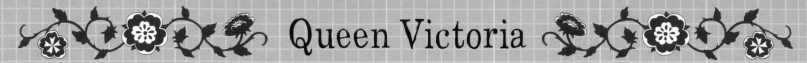
Victoria was a record-breaking monarch. She was the first queen to be photographed and filmed, and the first to have her head on postage stamps. She was queen of about one fifth of the world, and of almost a quarter of its people. By the end of her reign, Queen Victoria was hugely popular.

Her Golden and Diamond Jubilees were celebrated around the empire, and thousands of people crowded into London to watch her funeral in 1901. But not everyone liked her. She survived at least seven assassination attempts, including several shootings.

Here are the highlights of her reign:

A constitutional monarchy

Queen Victoria ruled for more than 63 years. Through her children and grandchildren, she was connected to almost every European royal house. However, she was a constitutional monarch, which meant she did not have the power to make decisions on how the country was run, and she was not allowed to change the law. But that did not always stop her from warning her ministers against doing things she did not approve of!

A fairer society

During Victoria's reign, life began to improve for ordinary people. More people than ever before were allowed to vote, while the 1842 Mines Act prevented women and children from working underground. An Education Act and a Public Health Act were passed by Parliament, and there were laws limiting the length of time anyone should work in the day to ten hours.

A dutiful queen

Victoria did her duty. She was active in state ceremonies and her family life and, together with her husband Albert, she was a model for the nation.

The Victorian Age

Victoria's reign spanned a time of enormous change: Britain had the world's biggest empire, the largest navy, and the most modern industries. Many places have been named after her: the state of Victoria in Australia; Lake Victoria and the Victoria Falls in Africa; the city of Victoria in Canada; and the Victoria Mountains in New Zealand are just some of her namesakes.

Glossary

dominion A territory, or country, under control of a supreme ruler, usually a monarch

empire A group of territories or countries under control of a supreme monarch

governess A women who is hired to care for, and teach, a child or children in a household

imperial The title of an emperor or empress

knickerbockers Loose fitting, short pants that gather below the knee

monarch A supreme ruler with a royal title of king, queen, emperor, or empress

petticoat A female undergarment worn under a skirt

reign A period of time in which a king or queen holds royal office

spats A cloth or leather shoe accessory that covers from the top of a shoe to behind the ankle

station A person's position in life

steward A person hired to manage a royal household

telegraph A device that sent messages by making and breaking electrical connections

truncheon A short club carried by a Victorian police officer

Viceroy A person hired as an authority on the behalf of a supreme ruler or monarch

Victorian Age The period of time that Queen Victoria reigned (1837-1901)

Index

Other characters in the Stories of Great People series.

SAFFRON sells pots and pans, herbs, spices, oils, soaps, and dyes from her spice kitchen set up under under a shady awning.

BUZZ is a street vendor with all the gossip. He sells candies from a tray that's strapped around his neck.

COLONEL KARBUNCLE sells military uniforms, medals, flags, swords, helmets, cannon balls—all from the trunk of his old jeep.

PRU is a dreamer and Hannah's best friend. She likes to visit the market with Digby and Hannah, especially when makeup and dressing up is involved.

JAKE is Digby's friend. He's got a lively imagination and is always up to mischief.

Mr. **POLLOCK**'s toy stall is filled with string puppets, rocking horses, model planes, wooden animals—and he makes them all himself!